Kierkegaard's Cupboard

To Stephen, Jonathan and Charlotte

Kierkegaard's Cupboard
Marianne Burton

Seren is the book imprint of
Poetry Wales Press Ltd.
57 Nolton Street, Bridgend, Wales, CF31 3AE
www.serenbooks.com
facebook.com/SerenBooks
twitter@SerenBooks

The right of Marianne Burton to be identified as
the author of this work has been asserted in accordance
with the Copyright, Designs and Patents Act, 1988

© Marianne Burton, 2018

ISBN: 978-1-78172-422-4
ebook: 978-1-78172-423-1
Kindle: 978-1-78172-424-8

A CIP record for this title is available from the British Library.

All rights reserved. No part of this publication may be reproduced,
stored in a retrieval system, or transmitted at any time or by any means,
electronic, mechanical, photocopying, recording or otherwise without
the prior permission of the copyright holder.

The publisher acknowledges the financial assistance of the Welsh Books Council.

Cover painting: Interior with Woman Reading (oil on panel), Carl Holsøe
(1863-1935) / Private Collection / Photo © Connaught Brown, London /
Bridgeman Images

Author photograph: © Barney Jones

Printed in Bembo by Bell & Bain Ltd, Scotland.

Contents

It is perfectly true, as the philosophers say, that life can only be understood backwards.
But they forget the other proposition, that it must be lived forwards.

Søren Aabye Kierkegaard – Journal 1843

How To Write A Preface

A preface is a mood.

It is tuning a guitar,
sharpening a scythe,
bowing invitingly at the start of a dance.

It is spitting from a window,
ringing a doorbell to run away,
swinging a stick to strike the wind,
passing a young girl's window staring at the road.

It is to pulse with longing for a quest to start.
It is to stand on Valby Hill gazing at the wild geese.
It is being alone without any fear of being alone.
It is having arrived at the beloved's house, sitting in the best chair
in the comfortable parlour, and having endless topics to converse upon.

It is to speak of all these things in a low whisper as night falls.

I. Childhood

Søren Aabye Kierkegaard was born on 5th May 1813, the youngest of seven children. All but two died before the age of 34. His relationship with his father, who suffered from a deep sense of guilt and melancholy, marked his life.

Kierkegaard is often described as 'the father of existentialism' for the emphasis he placed on the responsibility of the individual in determining his or her life's meaning and relationship with God. The individual is all, the crowd is untruth.

Echoes Fall In Strange Places

Echoes fall in strange places.
My father as a shepherd boy, so cold
he warmed his hands on dung, turned his face
to the sky and cursed an indifferent God.

My mother used to tell me not to whisper
about people in church. They cannot hear,
I said, they are either asleep or fixed on the pastor.
You never know who hears,
she said. Bad words travel faster
than good and make their nests in the wrong ears.

My father cried out in his sleep at night:
I did not mean it. Spare my children.
The sins of his melancholy love were blight
to our lives, but to my work they are foundation.

For A Long Time He Was Very Childish

School Evaluation for Søren Aabye Kierkegaard

For a long time he was very childish,
the most provoking and the least serious.

His small stature and death of a brother
may have caused some wariness of others,
but he is unspoilt, clever, merry and open,
and thoroughly versed in his religion.

Love of freedom and an occasionally amusing lack
of restraint prevents him embracing any topic
too deeply; he seems afraid if he commits it might
be difficult to pull back. But this tendency should abate.

There has been notable progress in the last year
and when the university allows his intellect to prosper
he will surely be counted a most able scholar
and come to resemble his elder brother.

I Have Just Returned From A Party

I have just returned from a party.

I was the life and soul; banter flowed
from my lips; everyone laughed, admired,
thought me happy, but I came away –
(make that dash as long as the radii of the earth's orbit)

───────────────────────────────

wanting to shoot myself.

I carry grief
embedded in my heart.

The only dignified revenge on the world
is to smile, entertain, keep your pain hidden.
Let other people tell you their misfortunes
and when they say you're blessed, the child
of luck, when no one sees your anguish,
that's success.

Of Course I Remember Uncle Søren

Of course I remember Uncle Søren.
He wrote funny letters that made us laugh.
He was always talking. He chatted to everyone
on his daily walks, he called them 'people baths'.

When his servant Anders called at our house
we knew something exciting was going to happen
and we would run round and round making a fuss
shrieking *Uncle Søren Uncle Søren*.

My best memory is my sister's birthday:
he brought us a pink cake with marzipan daisies
and gave us champagne and Mama was angry
and he drove us round the city for a surprise
though the only thing I remember about that
was a seal which had very big sad eyes.

My Umbrella, My Familiar

My umbrella, my familiar. So dear
I take it with me dazzle or drizzle, thunder or swelter.

To prove I do not love it merely for usefulness,
I sometimes stroll my rooms
and pretend that I am out.
I lean on it, put it up, bring it near my lips,
rest my chin upon its stalwart handle.

I have other umbrellas but I choose,
like men with dogs and horses,
to make this one my favourite.
The others do not mind.
They are pragmatic objects.
Not being loved exclusively
does not reduce their sense of self.

I Must Decide What To Do

Not

casting someone else's
vote, wearing someone else's

coat, singing someone else's
notes, mouthing lines I learnt

by rote. Something more than
loss or gain, something more than

keeping sane, something worth
the work and pain. Truth that rings

like truth for me, not out-worn
ontology. Not their religion

(since past thirty every man
should be his own pastor).

One truth for which I live and die.

It Is Sunday, The Best Day

It is Sunday, the best day,
the best month, July.

I am writing
and watching people walking
in the Frederiksberg Garden.
So many lovers, parents, children,

but I stand unfettered, a solitary
fir tree,
a spire
pointing higher, ever higher.

My body throws
no shadow.
Only the wild dove fashions
her nest in my branches.

II. Regine

In 1840 Kierkegaard became engaged to the beautiful, vibrant 17-year-old Regine Olsen, who fell deeply in love with him. After a year's engagement, to everyone's distress, Kierkegaard persuaded her that she must end the relationship, although he remained obsessed with her to the end of his life.

In 1843 Regine became engaged to her former tutor Frederik Schlegel and married him in November 1847, to Kierkegaard's dismay although he remained adamant that marriage with him was never a possibility.

When I Pass The Street Vendors Selling Herring

When I pass the street vendors selling herring
I am overwhelmed.
Luck seems to hang on choice.

I have seen the nets come home
flashing their silver, their miser's cache,
each pellet snapping and leaping against the next,
many as grains in a bushel,
many as graves in the yard.

Anxiety is the dizziness freedom spawns.
How should I pick just one?

In fairy tales the right fish holds the ring
one loved above all things but tossed into the sea.
The right fish will retrieve what one has lost.
How could one choose one, just one amongst so many?

Either / Or

Listen Søren / I said listen / Søren do as you want
/ marry the girl or don't / it's all the same /
even if she loves you today it won't
last past the first glad year or two / she'll blame
you for neglect whenever you try to read
or lock yourself up to write / she'll shame
you in front of the neighbours / claim you lead
her a dog's life with your incessant gloom /

and you / once you share washing facilities
with a woman all mystery is gone / the bloom
fades to ennui before the lover's eyes /
that's how it goes / boredom rules the bedroom
until decay / death's emissary / fucks your wife /
take her or don't / you'll regret both / that's life.

When She Stood There Clad
In Her Finery

when she stood there clad in her finery
i had to leave
when her delighted lively glance met mine
i had to leave
i went out and i wept bitterly

this muggy poultice soaked in sweat
that is the body and the body's pain
the fatigue of evening and the daylight's drain

i believe in the forgiveness of sins
but as i understand that doctrine
one must bear punishment in this world
for such a state of grace to be achieved

my punishment is loneliness and grief
the prison of the self

In August I Approached Her

In August I approached her.
In September I wooed her.
The next October I cast her from me
rather than we both be lost.

She claimed the split would kill her.
Then came the time of terror
when I had to turn her from me,
make her family hate me, to my cost.

Three people wrote my life:
one, a melancholy man,
two, a child-woman,
three, my close companion, grief.

Sadness is the best mistress, *fidelis semper*,
no wonder then that I return to her.

She Is Married –

She is married –
to whom I don't know because I dropped
the paper when I saw her name.
It came like a storm.

I am whole again. She has healed what was split.
The self that no one else would pick up off the street
is unified through her generosity.

Whoever she has chosen – I will not say preferred
because, as a husband, anyone is preferable to me –
she has acted, to me, generously.

Let her eyes dim, her beauty fade,
her curls lose their allure, her regal glance
that ruled the world embrace a quiet household –
a girl so generous will not grow old.

He Is Likeable

He is likeable.
And she believes herself happy. So much is truth.
But she is an instrument only I know
how to play. She is capable
of sounds only I know how
to summon forth.

She does not see
that I am looking
but she feels it through her full body.
She shuts her eyes to make it night
but within her it is daylight
and she feels the disrobing.

This was why it was then and how.
This is my final word on her. For now.

In This Palisander Cupboard

In this palisander cupboard I have placed
all the documents that made us what we were
when we were anything. I could not love lightly.
Everything I own will be yours. Believe me,
I would not have made a good husband.
Remember me kindly and be grateful
I chose not to spoil your life through marriage.

In the hush before dawn when carts rattle
over the cobbles I think of you. Then I rise,
eat breakfast, consider how as man and wife
we would have had to find some conversation
to orchestrate our eggs and ham. How banal
love becomes, the puddle in the gutter
one steps over keeping one's shoes clean.

III. The Writings

Kierkegaard wrote and published extensively from 1838 until his death. His books, essays and articles cover satire, fiction, theology, philosophy, psychology and literary criticism. They are frequently experimental in style, defying genre classification. He employed a number of pseudonyms, often humorous, such as Hilarius Bookbinder and Anti-Climacus.

To Kierkegaard, his most important writings were those in which he tried to interpret and revive the Christian faith and rescue it from what he felt was the stultifying hand of the state Lutheran Church.

Either/Or and *Fear and Trembling* are probably his two best-known works.

Either/Or was published in February 1843. It consists of several parts. One section, 'The Seducer's Diary', portrays the sensual life through the papers of a young man, the witty ironical disillusioned Johannes, recording his pursuit, seduction and desertion of Cordelia. Another presents the reflections of the middle-aged Judge William in praise of married love.

Fear and Trembling was published in October 1843. It considers, inter alia, different versions of the story of Abraham's proposed sacrifice of his son Isaac.

Kierkegaard was also a prolific journal keeper and a sensitive writer of letters.

A Good Answer Is Like A Sweet Kiss

My Cordelia

A good answer is like a sweet kiss
says Solomon.
As you know I have a weakness
for asking questions.
I have even been censured for this
by people who do not appreciate questions.

You and you alone understand my questions.
You and you alone understand why I seek answers.
You and you alone know how to give a good answer

for
as Solomon says
a good answer is like a sweet kiss.

Your Johannes

I Am In Love With Myself People Say

My Cordelia

I am in love with myself people say.
That does not surprise me.

How would it be possible for them to see
that I can love, that I do love, only you,

and therefore I love myself. Why?
Because I am in love with you

and everything of yours, and thus I love myself
because this self of mine belongs to you.

If I stopped loving you, I would unlove myself.
What seems to the profane world pure egotism

is in fact, as you alone can see, an expression
of the most inspired self-obliteration.

Your Johannes

Something Wonderful Happened Yesterday

Something wonderful happened yesterday.
I left for heaven. The old gods summoned me.
Mercury said, 'Various gifts we have to give away:
power, long life, the loveliest women, beauty.
Choose – but only one.'
                            Bewildered, I considered.
Then I knew. I bowed with gratitude and pride.
'My esteemed contemporaries', I said,
'I would like laughter always on my side.'

Silent and still they sat, straight-faced.
Then laughter started, swelling with relish.
From which I guessed they granted my request.
Gods are good stylists. They know best
how to express themselves. It would have been bad taste
to give solemn assent to such a wish.

Many Men Agree With Byron's Declaration

Many men agree with Byron's declaration
that marriage is hell, though love is heaven.

But if marriage has its foe in time,
it has its triumph in time.
It is romantic love's best manifestation,
its transfiguration, not annihilation.

If love is present when engagement is entered into, it will not stale.
If the beauty of the pagan erotic is kept alive, it will not stale.
If first love's renewal is not recollection but action, it will not stale.

It can confound the scoffers, outflank the envious.

Marriage has music dear to the man who knows its truth
like a stream where you used to swim
which sings of your youth.

It is only the new which grows tedious.

It Was Early Morning. Abraham Rose

It was early morning. Abraham rose,
had the donkeys saddled, left his tents,
rode away with Isaac. Sarah watched
until nothing stayed of them but absence.

Three days they rode. Silence. Desert.
Abraham raised his eyes, took Isaac's hand,
bade the servants wait, and climbed Mount Moriah,
a knife at his hip. Isaac did not understand.

Then Abraham shook the boy savagely:
This is my wish for blood, not God's order.
And the boy cried: *Lord my protector save me
from my father the murderer.*

Better he believes I am a monster
than that he should lose faith in thee.

It Was Early Morning. Abraham Rose

It was early morning. Abraham rose,
embraced Sarah, bride of his autumn,
who kissed Isaac, child of her hope,
then they rode away. Eyes down. Dumb.

Abraham kept his gaze on the cold soil

silently he lit the wood
silently he bound his child
silently he drew the knife
saw the ram
took its life
went home.

From that day Abraham grew old.
He could not forget God's instruction.
Isaac throve but Abraham's joy was gone.

It Was Early Morning. Abraham Rose

It was early morning. Abraham rose,
kissed Sarah, the mother, and Sarah
kissed Isaac, her delight for ever.

As Abraham rode, he thought of Hagar
and their son driven into the wilderness.

They climbed the mountain.
He drew the knife.

It was a quiet evening when Abraham rode alone
to Mount Moriah. He threw himself down
and prayed for forgiveness for offering Isaac's life.

He could not believe it was a sin
to offer God the best thing
he possessed. And he would not believe
God might forgive.

It Was Early Morning. Everything Was Packed

It was early morning. Everything was packed.
Abraham took tender leave of Sarah.
Isaac stood ready. Their servant Eleazor
rode out with them before turning back.

Father and son rode with one accord. Calmly quietly.

Calmly quietly Abraham prepared to take Isaac's life
but as he turned his face away
Isaac saw his father's left hand clenched in agony
a shudder through his body
as he drew the knife.

Sarah ran to kiss them back to their routine.
But Isaac's faith was lost.
Isaac told no one what he had witnessed
and Abraham did not suspect he had been seen.

When The Child Is To Be Weaned

When the child is to be weaned
the mother blackens her breast

so the child believes the breast
has changed but not the mother,

for her look is tender and loving
as ever. Her heart is not black.

When the child is to be weaned
the mother covers her breast

and the mother sorrows to lose
the child who lay beneath her heart.

When the child is to be weaned
the mother offers solid food.

Lucky the child who loses his mother
in no other way. Who is offered other food.

Lord Jesus Christ, You Did Not Come Into The World

Lord Jesus Christ, you did not come into the world
to be worshipped like a modern Apollo or Dagon,
admired like a soldier in uniform strutting down the road,
served like a supercilious politician.
We must imitate your love. That is all you asked.

The New Testament is very easy to understand
but we Christians are a bunch of swindlers
who pretend we do not understand.
We are a bunch of self-deceivers,
because we know the minute we do understand

we will be obliged to act. How awkward.
Easier to sleep on, face down in our mutton stew.
It is dreadful to be alone with you,
dreadful to fall into the hands of the living God.

There Is An Indescribable Joy

There is an indescribable joy
that rises of itself
that takes in the city
and the city's thought

as when a sudden gust of wind
breaks the string
and the kite staggers away
not in a horizontal flick
but perpendicular
as though fall
were impossible
up until perspective
shrinks it out of sight.

Imagine how we look from there.

IV. After *The Corsair*

In 1846 *The Corsair*, a satirical journal, began to lampoon Kierkegaard through drawings and articles, mocking his writing, appearance, clothes and habits, and even his relationship with Regine. Kierkegaard was no longer able to walk through Copenhagen or its outskirts without being hounded and laughed at as a figure of fun.

Regine and Kierkegaard began to pass each other on their daily walks. They acknowledged each other with nods and smiles but never spoke. In 1849 Kierkegaard wrote to Frederik Schlegel enclosing a letter for Regine, asking if he might meet and talk to her in Schlegel's presence, or correspond if Schlegel read their letters. Several drafts of Kierkegaard's letters exist. Schlegel refused.

In March 1855 Schlegel was appointed Governor of the Danish West Indies for five years. On her last day in Copenhagen Regine wished Kierkegaard well as they passed.

Kierkegaard dedicated his life's work to Regine.

I Am Become A Caricature

I am become a caricature, a parody.
Every morning nursemaids send their children
to call *Magister Søren Magister Søren*
tell us the time. Then they laugh and run away.

My tailor suggests I take my trade elsewhere.
For, he says, my thin legs and high shoulders
make a travesty of his clothes and he loses
business through my patronage. Thank you, *Corsair.*

My nephew, who often strides by my side
for a few blocks sharing childish talk,
saw me, saw the street lads point and gawk,
then crossed and took another path. He lied
to me later, said he hadn't seen me on his walk.
Well, better men than I have been denied.

To Them Normality Is The Highest Good

To them normality is the highest good,
better than intelligence. They have never
felt nostalgia for the mysterious,
the far-away, never felt the pleasure

of being nobody, free of meetings,
strolling through the North Gate out of town
with pennies in one's pocket, carrying
nothing but a slender bamboo cane.

They are men who like only other men like them:
jeerers, whorers, drinkers. Normal as migraine,
as ill-fitting windows, as winter's mucky hem.

They pass the broken door, the half-drawn blind.
They never hear the crying, see the pain
their jeering and their whoring leave behind.

Esteemed Sir, The Enclosed Letter Is From Me (S. Kierkegaard)

Draft of a letter sent to Frederik Schlegel November 1849

Esteemed Sir, the enclosed letter is from me (S. Kierkegaard)
to – your wife. You must decide whether to pass it on to her.

My personality once affected her powerfully and rather
than risk it proving too strong again and disturbing her

I decided to write to you. I thought this the wiser course,
despite having had many opportunities for discourse.

I would like to meet her with you there. Or if you think it better
we could correspond with you double-signing all her letters.

The girl's worth was quite extraordinary. I had to make her unhappy
and out of that grief I became an author. She was unhappy through me

and out of that grief I have embraced in her name inhuman exertion
and have as an author sought out dangers all others shun.

In this life she stands by your side, but in history she belongs to me.
You make her happy in this life – I will see to her immortality.

He Returns Her Letter

The letter sent to Regine Schlegel is returned, unopened

He returns her letter and takes the trouble
of reading me a moral lecture. It was due to me he had her.
Due to me he has her now. One word and I could have her back.

I am the guardian of his marriage and he treats me with disdain.

It is ~~impossible~~ difficult to speak to her now.
My voice might awaken echoes of past passion.

Thank you Regina for the time when you were mine
thank you for your childlike trust
my bird of the air
my lily of the field
my teacher from whom I learned so much.

I hope you will consider I have honestly observed what I promised
when you asked at our parting if I would think of you

now and then.

Above All, Jette, Do Not Forget To Walk

Letter to his brother's wife who suffered poor health

Above all, Jette, do not forget to walk.
I have walked myself into all my best thoughts
and I know no thought so burdensome
that I cannot walk away from it.
Every day I walk myself into a state of well-being
and away from illness.
I promise, it is possible.

People say 'keep faith', but what does that mean?
It is to believe good things can happen,
to change each day's dejection into anticipation of joy.
Whenever things go wrong
in that very instant begin again
and say to your disheartened self:
Yes! Yes! Next time it will work.

Remember To Love Yourself

Letter to Hans Peter, his crippled cousin

Remember to love yourself.

You may have been set apart from life,
have been prevented from participating
in any active sense, which may cause you grief.

You may be seen as superfluous
in the eyes of this world, which is unthinking,

as if a life lived in inwardness
did not have as much worth and sense
as that of any other human being
in the eyes of the all-wise all-seeing Governance

and considerably more worth
than those busy business behemoths
who rush about spending other people's lives,
flashing their cash, and losing their own selves.

The Better The Book The Fewer
The Readers

The better the book the fewer the readers.
Yet how critics drip their rancid honey
after two oily words in their vain ears:
Read Amazing Mr X, Talented Dr Y,

the real, the exciting, the raging genius.
The worse the writing, the more reviewers shout.
Books, of course, are only mirrors:
if an ape looks in, no apostle will look out.

But what else can one do?
As the assassins in Scheherazade's
chamber were gestured to return tomorrow,
as next night again their swords were paused
from cutting off her voice, and on and on, so do
I save myself and keep myself alive through words.

Not Until Hope Has Been Thrown Overboard

Not until Hope has been thrown overboard
does one's artistic life take up its oars.

It is a splendid sight when someone's boat,
fresh wind in its sails, pulls out dawn-washed
with jaunty inexperience singing at the helm.
But he who trusts his ship to Hope is lost.

She neglects the maps and instruments
that pessimism checks obsessively.
She forgets to test her limitations
because every endeavour seems so jolly.

Prometheus gave man many gifts
– disobedience, fire, choice cuts of meat –
but Hope is best squeezed into a chest
and weighed down several thousand fathoms deep.

There Are Two Degrees Of War

There are two degrees of war.

Imagine the street:
two dogs begin to fight.
Heads peer out and from two doors
the women come who own the dogs.

A new fight starts.
The husbands of the women come.
Then onlookers pile in
pulling each other's clothes
claiming they know which dog bit first
and which dog snarled before.

War in the first degree is war.
War in the second degree is war
about who started the first war.

If Christ Returned Into The World

If Christ returned into the world
he would be kissed into betrayal
by the press. He would be mocked
through cartoons and handed over to ridicule.

If Christ returned into the world
he would spare the money changers and bird traders
and take up whips against the newspapers.

I am not bloodthirsty
but given absolute certainty
that all those up against the wall were
journalists, I myself would give the word to fire.

Of course, one sometimes has to wield those weapons
the world wields. Sometimes one has to threaten
those who threatened first. To stoop. Just for a moment.

V. *The Moment*

From December 1854 Kierkegaard published a series of articles in the newspaper *The Fatherland* criticising the Danish Lutheran Church and its chief ministers for being too materialistic, too intrusive and overly state-controlled.

From May 1855 he continued this intense attack in a series of self-published tracts under the title *The Moment*.

Nine issues were published before Kierkegaard fell ill in September.

Imagine A Hospital Where Patients Die Like Flies

Imagine a hospital where patients die like flies.

Fatalities are listed, one from this disease,
one from that infection. The dying doesn't halt
when treatments change. It's the building's fault.
Death seeps grinning out of brick and drain and slate.

So with religion. Our toxic wreck of a state
Church is the poisoner. Unaired for generations,
it needs the correction of persecution not protection.

Look. In the splendid cathedral
in his fine robes the right honourable
royal chaplain steps forward to discourse,
deeply moved, upon his favourite verse:
God honours the lowly and scornéd of the earth.
No one roars with mirth.

A Young Man Has No Need Of Religion

A young man has no need of religion
but as a father he is obliged to sign in
if he wants to bestow a civic education.

That's when a silk-clad pastor jumps in sight,
talking about another soldier for the fight,
sprinkling water, insisting on the Church's rights.

And one dares to offer this as Christian baptism?
The solemn ceremony offering up one's life?
Do you think God is a fool? Stick a wax nose on him
and have done with it.
                        Leave birth to the midwife.
Leave children innocent, unchurched, unafraid.
But of course this is not about religion but money.
Before the baptism, money; before the sick call, money;
before the funeral, money. Every man a thief in his own trade.

The Difference Between The Theatre And The Church

The difference between the theatre and the Church
is essentially this: the theatre does not pretend.
The theatre is open, the Church covert.
Theatre posters say no money will be returned

if the show's a dud, but the Church would shrink
from the offensiveness, the scandal, of hanging this
above the door, printing it on the preacher list.
Who then is the rogue? Who the truth witness?

But don't get the idea that pastors are actors
while we are critics, doling out blame or praise.
No, we are the actors: preachers merely prompters.
God is our audience. Even on slow days –
no ticket sold, no seat warmed by a friendly arse –
he sits in the stalls, smiles, weeps at our farce.

When Fire Breaks Out, What Does The Fire Chief Say?

When fire breaks out, what does the fire chief say?
When helpful neighbours run up with a patio spray
and garden pail and jug? He is an affable
fellow, soft-spoken and kind. Does he thank people?

He calls the police, and when they come, he shouts,
'You lazy bums, get these stupid half-wits out,
they're blocking the engines. And if politeness
doesn't shift their carcasses, kick some ass.'

Well, it's the same when fires need starting.
Neighbourly citizens with sulphurless
matches and damp tapers begin farting
around. Leave it to us, the arsonists.
Gasp as our incendiary pens shoot fire-larks
soaring into the corners of your dark.

Let Me Tell You Some Stories About Geese

Let me tell you some stories about geese.
One about a wild goose who tried to teach
the fat farm geese to fly. That didn't end well.

Or one about some farm geese who wanted to fly,
who grew fit practising. The others watched them try,
'How thin and ill they look. How irresponsible.'

Or one about the fattest goose who on Sundays
hopped on to the trough singing *every day's your birthday
in the farmyard*, preaching how warm and safe and lucky
farm geese are, how blessèd is the state of Goosedom.
When wild geese flew overhead, the farm geese felt numb
for a few moments, depressed by a sense of boredom.
They flapped, thought of the terrible Christmas inevitability,
but the fattest goose had to be right. His words, his weight, his wisdom…

When You Are Depressed
You Become Reckless

When you are depressed you become reckless.
You forget the tenderness you owe yourself.
You become a body you don't recognise.

Like the peasant who went into town to buy
shoes and stockings and had some money
left to get drunk before lurching home. On his way
he fell over, fell asleep, lay like a felled tree

until woken by a driver bellowing,
'Get off the road or I'll run over your legs.'
The peasant looked down at his new stockings
and shouted, 'That's fine by me. They're not my legs.'

We look strange because we expect our self
to be fixed whereas it keeps on growing.
You are your own child. Tend it. Guard its health.

Smell Of Smoke. Flames Lick The Backdrop

Smell of smoke. Flames lick the backdrop.
Into the crowded theatre a clown runs, 'Fire. Stop
the show. Evacuate immediately.'

The audience loves the gag. It screams with glee.

The clown shouts louder, 'You must leave now.'
The audience catcalls, wobbles its beery jowls.

The clown begs them. He is in tears.

The audience laughs itself to fits. It cheers
the clown's growing desperation, claps, elbows friends.

And this is the way the world ends.
No bangs, no whimpers,
just loud-mouthed humour
among clever folk
who think the warning is a joke.

I Am Not A Christian

I am not a Christian.
That statement is very awkward for the sophists
who want me to proclaim myself the only Christian,
declare myself with drums and trumpets.

I do not call myself a Christian
and that makes it difficult to get rid of me.
Saying I am not a Christian
makes it clear the others are even more paltry.

No. I am not the physician. I am one of the sick.
Worse, I am the slip of the pen that has become self-conscious
and rebels against the author.

No. I will not be deleted.
I remain here as witness
that you are a second-rate writer.

VI. Death

Kierkegaard checked himself into hospital on 2nd October 1855 after several falls.

He was in hospital for forty-one days suffering from creeping paralysis from the feet up. He was aware that he was dying, having exhausted himself financially, emotionally and physically. Meticulous medical records were kept, but no reason for his illness could be established. Joakim Garff's biography suggests modern medical analysis might indicate a progressive neurological disease such as Guillain-Barré syndrome.

Kierkegaard died, aged forty-two, on 11th November 1855.

Not A Day Without A Line

not a day without a line
for to forget to write is to forget one has a mind

not a day without walking
for to forget to walk is to forget one has a body

not a day without prayer
for to forget to pray is to forget one has a soul

not a day without conversation
for to forget to talk is to forget one has compassion

not a day without memory
for to forget to remember is to forget one has a past

not a day without regret
for to forget one's loss is to forget one has been loved

not a day without tears
for to forget one loved is to forget one lived

My Misfortune From Birth Was Not
To Be Wholly Human

My misfortune from birth was not to be wholly human.
From childhood I was trained to obey,
strictly educated, drilled in religion,
given every advantage except being free
to slip out of depression for a single day.

I was not like the others, something I so wanted to be.
A man can endure being a glorious oddity, the uncommon,
but for a boy and a youth it is agony.

I was turned the wrong way out, like a sock rolled
waiting to be pulled on. I went into life, pursued
enjoyment enjoying nothing. I was fun's outcast.

I have no immediacy and in the sense of being fully human
I have never lived. I did not learn reflection,
I am reflection from first to last.

The Head Nurse Writes. She Sent Me A Play Once

The head nurse writes. She sent me a play once.
I don't think I replied but when one is dying
one cannot remember all one's correspondence.
She supervises the hospital during the daytime

and my room at night. She brought flowers for me
and placed them in water. Let them be,
I said, flowers should bloom, be fragrant, and then die.
The night staff say that while I sleep she cries.

How quiet dying is. Like the greatest hazard
of all, losing the self, which often happens quietly
in the world, as if it were nothing.
No other mislaying occurs so quietly.
Any other loss, an arm, a leg, a ring,
five dollars or a wife, is sure to be noticed.

A Stream Ran Beside My Father's Farm

A stream ran beside my father's farm
who always played with me.
She never aged though I grew old, never lost purity.

Her tranquil steadiness never denied me
what people tried to deny me by making eternity
as busy and more terrible than time.

She stayed with me when I needed an eternity
to forget, I was so sad; when I needed an eternity
to rest, I was so tired of people, so tired of who I am.

And God is like that stream but better, infinitely,
because his stream travels searching for the thirsty.

No one strays so far he cannot remember the way
home, at whatever age at whatever time of day,
to the stream's cool, to the warmth of his father's farm.

The Sword Is Too Sharp For The Scabbard

Thin and delicate, denied physicality,
sick in my mind and melancholy,
a failure in many ways, profoundly and ostensibly,
I was given one thing:

                      an astute mind, presumably
to keep me from being completely
defenceless. My truth weapon.

                                Already
as a young boy I was aware of its dexterity.

Müller says there are two great entities
around which everything revolves: women and ideas.
Most run after women and forget the ideas;
in my case it took a girl to get the ideas
whetted and cutting true. An unusual case.

Well, the sword is too sharp for the scabbard.
It has worn it out.

I Will Be Understood After My Death

I will be understood after my death. I have not been understood
but God understood me and I understood myself.
That must suffice.

I will be studied after my death. The time will come when my writings
and my entire life will be studied, the whole machinery.
That must suffice.

I have been disliked but that is what the New Testament predicts.
My detractors will decorate my grave,
say we respected him although no one else respected him.
That must suffice.

I was not what the times perhaps craved, a reformer, a prophet, a seer,
but I had a definite talent for detection.
I was an honest bloodhound on the beat.
And that must suffice.

Close The Hatch, That's What The Old Hymn Says

Close the hatch, that's what the old hymn says.
Close the hatch that is the coffin lid, make it tight
so I can find peace like a child who is happy when hidden.

Close the hatch, make it really tight. I am not there,
just what I so wanted to be rid of, this body of sin,
this House of Correction uniform I was forced to wear.

I am still out over seventy thousand fathoms of water,
still preserving my faith, still practising my shout of joy,
never forgetting that God is my helper
and my final wish is that everything shall serve to his glory

before I take the path we must all take
across the Bridge of Sighs into eternity.

Close the hatch close it tight
really tight.

Author's Note & Acknowledgements

This is not a work of scholarship or translation. Some poems are more Kierkegaard's than mine and vice versa. Perhaps the best way to describe this book is that it is a personal interpretation, in the same way that jazz interpretations pay homage to standards. I apologise to Kierkegaard scholars for extensive liberties taken; so, as one example, the passage about a stream which Kierkegaard gives to Constantin Constantius is here given to Kierkegaard himself. Since Kierkegaard often mentions swimming and water with affection and since Copenhagen is a water city, I feel this remains true to his spirit. I hope at least that anyone reading this book with no knowledge of Kierkegaard's life and works should feel by the end they have a grasp of what he ventured. I hope readers will go on to read proper books about him. This is a book of poetry and as such is not at all proper.

I have read many translations of Kierkegaard's works and many books and websites about his life over the years. The books to which I am most indebted are Howard V. Hong and Edna H. Hong's translations of Kierkegaard's writings from the Princeton University Press and Joakim Garff's *Søren Kierkegaard: a biography*, translated by Bruce H. Kirmmse (2007 edition: Princeton). Also, *Kierkegaard: Letters and Documents* translated by Henrik Rosenmeier (1978: Princeton); *Written Images* by Niels Jørgen Cappelørn, Joakim Garff and Johnny Kondrup, translated by Bruce H. Kirmmse (2003: Princeton); *Fear and Trembling*, translated by Alastair Hannay (1985: Penguin); *Søren Kierkegaard: papers and journals: a selection,* edited and translated by Alastair Hannay (1996: Penguin); and *The Oxford Handbook of Kierkegaard* by John Lippitt, George Pattison and others (2013: Oxford). I have made a poor attempt with a dictionary at reading Peter Tudvad's *Kierkegaards København* (2004: Politiken). I should also mention M.G. Piety's blog, D. Anthony Storm's website, Joakim Garff's *Kierkegaard's Muse: The Mystery of Regine Olsen* translated by Alastair Hannay (2017: Princeton), and the Søren Kierkegaard Archive at the Royal Library, Denmark.

I should like to thank Malene Engelund for helping me with Danish and the Museum of Copenhagen for showing me their Kierkegaard collection, including the cupboard. Acknowledgement is due to *Ambit* and *Poetry Review* in which some of these poems first appeared.